FENG SHUI
KUA DIRECTIONS

FENG SHUI KUA DIRECTIONS

BY LORETA CILFONE

Feng Shui Kua Directions
The formula to find your good and bad directions revealed

Copyright © 2016 Loreta Cilfone. All rights reserved.

First Published 2016 by: Conscious Care Publishing Pty Ltd
33 Crompton Road, Rockingham, WA 6168, Australia
PO Box 776, Rockingham, WA 6968, Australia
Phone: (61+) 1300 814 115   www.consciouscarepublishing.com.au

First Edition printed August 2016.

Notice of Rights
This book is sold subject to the condition that it shall not, by way of trade or otherwise, be lent, resold, hired out, or otherwise circulated without the publisher's prior consent, in any form of binding or cover, other than that in which it is published, and without a similar condition, including this condition being imposed on the subsequent purchaser. All rights reserved by the publisher. No part of this publication may be reproduced, stored in a retrieval system, or transmitted in any form, or by any means, electronic, digital, mechanical, photocopying, scanning, recorded or otherwise, without the prior written permission of the copyright owner. Requests to the copyright owner should be addressed to Permissions Department, Conscious Care Publishing Pty Ltd, PO Box 776, Rockingham, WA 6968, Australia, Phone: (61+) 8 9592 2004 or email rights@consciouscarepublishing.com.au

Categories
1. New Age. 2. Mind, Body, Spirit

Limits of Liability/Disclaimer of Warranty:
While the publisher and author have used their best efforts in preparing this book, they make no representations or warranties with respect to the accuracy or completeness of the contents of this book and specifically disclaim any implied warranties of merchantability or fitness for a particular purpose. No warranty may be created or extended by sales representatives or written sales materials. The author of this book does not dispense medical advice or prescribe the use of any technique as a form of treatment for physical, emotional, or medical problems without the advice of a physician, either directly or indirectly. The advice and strategies contained herein may not be suitable for your situation. You should consult with a professional where appropriate. The intent of the author is only to offer information for a general nature to help you in your request for a happier life. Neither the publisher nor author shall be liable for any loss of profit or any other commercial damages, including but not limited to special, incidental, consequential, or other damages. The author and the publisher assume no responsibility for your actions.

Conscious Care Publishing publishes in a variety of print and electronic format and by print-on-demand. Some material included with standard print versions of this book may not be included in e-books or in print-on-demand. If this book refers to media such as a CD or DVD that is not included in the version you purchased, you may download this material at http://consciouscarepublishing.com.au.

National Library of Australia Cataloguing-in-Publication entry:
Author: Cilfone, Loreta, 1974 -
Feng Shui Kua Directions : The formula to find your good and bad directions revealed / by Loreta Cilfone
ISBN 9780994540423 (Paperback)
Cilfone, Loreta, 1974 -
Rocky Hudson, Editor
Perth Branding & Marketing - Typeset Design
Printed by Lightning Source
133.3337

Dedicated to Benita,
just because.

CONTENTS

CHAPTER 1
Introduction — 09

CHAPTER 2
How to calculate your Kua number — 19

CHAPTER 3
Representations of Kua numbers — 29

CHAPTER 4
Kua number directions — 43

CHAPTER 5
Using your Kua number for sitting and sleeping — 55

CHAPTER 6
Using your Kua number for business — 65

CHAPTER 7
Your Kua number in relation to your home — 73

CHAPTER 8
Kua Directions family reference — 81

CHAPTER 1
INTRODUCTION

WHAT IS FENG SHUI?

Originating thousands of years ago in China, Feng Shui is an in-depth study in balancing energy in your living and work environments to bring about health, wealth and happiness. It helps us to live in peace and harmony.

The nature of Chi affects our health, relationships, and general success in any endeavour.

Energy in Feng Shui is known as 'Chi', and in any environment it can be either good or bad. The nature of the Chi affects our health, relationships, and general success in any endeavour.

Being in a happy and free-flowing environment which energy can meander through is good – it brings about positive Feng Shui. Unhappiness, negativity and obstructions in your environment bring about stale energy. It blocks good Feng Shui from taking place and it can result in bad luck, bad relationships, illness, and general hindrances.

Of all the Feng Shui Schools, Kua Directions is the easiest to implement without too much effort.

There are a few Schools of Feng Shui and this is why Feng Shui can often be overwhelming and perhaps difficult to understand.

This book looks at the basic use of Feng Shui Kua Directions.

WHAT ARE KUA DIRECTIONS?

Of all the Feng Shui Schools, Kua Directions is the easiest to implement without too much effort. Neither a floor plan nor Feng Shui products are required. You simply need to be aware of the eight compass locations (North, North East, East, South East, South, South West, West, North West) in relation to your home. You can also extend the use of your Kua Directions to your work premises, or anywhere you go.

If you are not aware of where the compass locations are in relation to your surroundings, most Smartphones have a compass utility, or a compass app you can download.

Using your Kua Directions is an easy and fantastic way for Feng Shui to start working for you immediately.

HOW KUA NUMBERS WORK

Based on your year of birth, you have a 'Kua' number. Kua numbers are: 1, 2, 3, 4, 6, 7, 8 and 9 (there is no Kua number 5). Your individual Kua number gives you four favourable directions and four unfavourable directions – relating to compass directions. Each of the eight directions has a representation.

For the best results in any endeavour, you want to ensure you are always facing one of your four favourable directions. Tapping in to your Kua favourable directions is most commonly used to position beds, office desks and study desks.

However, you can literally take advantage of your Kua Directions for anything, such as choosing which direction to face in meetings, during work presentations, when speaking in public, when asking for a pay rise, when you are on a date, or when you are out for breakfast, lunch or dinner. You can use them for any situation!

CHAPTER 2
HOW TO CALCULATE YOUR KUA NUMBER

WEST AND EAST GROUP CLASSIFICATIONS

Kua numbers are classified into two groups: West and East. Kua numbers belonging to the West Group are 2, 6, 7 and 8, with favourable directions of West, South West, North West and North East.

Kua numbers belonging to the East Group are 1, 3, 4 and 9, with favourable directions of East, South East, North and South.

Even though there are two group classifications, each direction of each Kua number has a different representation, which will be explained shortly.

CALCULATING YOUR KUA NUMBER

Let us use 1974 as an example. Discard numbers 1 and 9, and add numbers 7 and 4, which equals 11. Add 1 and 1, which equals 2. Then, if you are female, you add 5, to give a total of 7. Your Kua number is therefore 7.

If you are male, still using 1974 as an example, once you reach the step of adding 1 plus 1, equalling 2, you deduct 10, to give a total of -8. Your Kua number is therefore 8 (you ignore any minuses).

Note to keep reducing your end number to a single digit if required. For example, for a female born in 1980, discard numbers 1 and 9, add numbers 8 and 0, which equals 8. Then add 5, which equals 13. Then add 1 and 3, which equals 4. Your Kua number is therefore 4.

IF YOUR END RESULT IS KUA NUMBER 5

There is an exception to the rule – there is no Kua number 5. If once you have done your calculation your end number is 5, for females change it to Kua number 8, and for males change it to Kua number 2. It is that simple!

BORN IN THE YEAR 2000 AND BEYOND

The formula is different for people born in the year 2000 and beyond. Once you add the last two digits and break it down to one number, for a female you add 6, for a male you deduct 9. For example, for a female born in the year 2000; ignore the first two digits of 2 and 0, and you add the last two digits of 0 and 0, which equals 0, plus 6 equals 6. This person's Kua number is 6. For a male born in the year 2015, ignore the first two digits of 2 and 0, and you add 1 and 5 which equals 6, then deducting 9 equals -3. This person's Kua number is therefore 3.

BORN BEFORE 12 NOON, 4TH FEBRUARY

There is one final thing to note when working out a Kua number. Feng Shui works on the Chinese calendar which runs from 4th February to 4th February. If you were born before 12 noon on 4th February (in any year), you calculate your Kua number based on the previous year. For example, if you were born on 3rd January, 1982, you calculate your Kua number on the year 1981.

To simplify it for you, I have included tables for both females and males on the following pages, whereby the Kua numbers have already been calculated.

TABLE OF KUA NUMBERS FOR FEMALES

Remember to take in to consideration if you were born before 12 noon, 4th February.

KUA NUMBERS FOR FEMALES							
YEAR	KUA NO.	YEAR	KUA NO.	YEAR	KUA NO.	YEAR	KUA NO.
1940	9	1960	2	1980	4	2000	6
1941	1	1961	3	1981	8	2001	7
1942	2	1962	4	1982	6	2002	8
1943	3	1963	8	1983	7	2003	9
1944	4	1964	6	1984	8	2004	1
1945	8	1965	7	1985	9	2005	2
1946	6	1966	8	1986	1	2006	3
1947	7	1967	9	1987	2	2007	4
1948	8	1968	1	1988	3	2008	8
1949	9	1969	2	1989	4	2009	6
1950	1	1970	3	1990	8	2010	7
1951	2	1971	4	1991	6	2011	8
1952	3	1972	8	1992	7	2012	9
1953	4	1973	6	1993	8	2013	1
1954	8	1974	7	1994	9	2014	2
1955	6	1975	8	1995	1	2015	3
1956	7	1976	9	1996	2	2016	4
1957	8	1977	1	1997	3	2017	8
1958	9	1978	2	1998	4	2018	6
1959	1	1979	3	1999	8	2019	7

TABLE OF KUA NUMBERS FOR MALES

Remember to take in to consideration if you were born before 12 noon, 4th February.

KUA NUMBERS FOR MALES							
YEAR	KUA NO.	YEAR	KUA NO.	YEAR	KUA NO.	YEAR	KUA NO.
1940	6	1960	4	1980	2	2000	9
1941	2	1961	3	1981	1	2001	8
1942	4	1962	2	1982	9	2002	7
1943	3	1963	1	1983	8	2003	6
1944	2	1964	9	1984	7	2004	2
1945	1	1965	8	1985	6	2005	4
1946	9	1966	7	1986	2	2006	3
1947	8	1967	6	1987	4	2007	2
1948	7	1968	2	1988	3	2008	1
1949	6	1969	4	1989	2	2009	9
1950	2	1970	3	1990	1	2010	8
1951	4	1971	2	1991	9	2011	7
1952	3	1972	1	1992	8	2012	6
1953	2	1973	9	1993	7	2013	2
1954	1	1974	8	1994	6	2014	4
1955	9	1975	7	1995	2	2015	3
1956	8	1976	6	1996	4	2016	2
1957	7	1977	2	1997	3	2017	1
1958	6	1978	4	1998	2	2018	9
1959	2	1979	3	1999	1	2019	8

CHAPTER 3
REPRESENTATIONS OF KUA NUMBERS

WHAT THE KUA NUMBERS MEAN

Let us now take a look at the representation of the four favourable directions and the four unfavourable directions. All of the directions have an order in which they are written relating to their representations.

The way in which a direction relates specifically to you will depend on your Kua number. They all bring a different kind of energy.

Note that the directions following are not numbered incorrectly, this is the order of favourable and unfavourable depiction.

Favourable Kua Directions are:

1. Success and prosperity
2. Good health – strengthens the body and mind
3. Love and relationships
4. Personal growth – education, knowledge and wisdom.

Unfavourable Kua Directions are:

4. General bad luck – mishaps, setbacks and disappointments
3. Harmful people in your life – gossip and plotting against you
2. Misfortune in your life – accidents, wealth, and illness
1. Total loss in your life – bankruptcy, long term illness and major disaster.

SUCCESS AND PROSPERITY

Your success and prosperity direction is the ultimate direction when it comes to achieving success relating to wealth, and triumph in endeavours. Positioning your work desk so that you are facing this direction will energise you to achieve optimum results. Your career success will be boosted, your income will increase, and rewards in general will start to show.

Your success and prosperity direction is the ultimate direction when it comes to achieving success relating to wealth, and triumph in endeavours.

This position is commonly used for office desk set-up, giving a presentation, going for a job interview, and even asking for a pay rise.

GOOD HEALTH – STRENGTHENS THE BODY AND MIND

If your health seems to continually be undermined it is important to sleep in your good health direction. If you are always feeling sluggish, do not have much strength, and struggle in general on a health level, sleeping in this direction will help strengthen your body and mind. It is also a good direction to sit facing at the dinner table, as food is nourishing and gives us strength.

LOVE AND RELATIONSHIPS

If you are missing that special someone in your life, or simply wish to improve your current relationship, try sleeping in your love and relationships direction. Romance will enter your life, or enhance your existing relationship. This direction is also the best direction to sit facing when you are on a date. Your date will find you more desirable – just be sure that is what you want! You can also face this direction when you are simply talking to your partner, and it will produce a more harmonious conversation.

PERSONAL GROWTH – EDUCATION, KNOWLEDGE AND WISDOM

Your personal growth direction is the best direction in which to set up your study desk. Facing this direction while studying will help you think clearly and concisely, achieve your desired results for learning, and in general guide you along your path. It is an inspiring position to face and will advance your abilities. It is also a great direction to face if you are trying to wind down and relax. If you are soul searching, sleeping in this direction will assist in this endeavour.

Your personal growth direction is the best direction in which to set up your study desk.

GENERAL BAD LUCK – MISHAPS, SETBACKS AND DISAPPOINTMENTS

Of the four unfavourable directions, the general bad luck direction is the least unfavourable – that is to say the least damaging. It does, however, bring all kinds of minor mishaps, setbacks and disappointments.

HARMFUL PEOPLE IN YOUR LIFE – GOSSIP AND PLOTTING AGAINST YOU

The official Chinese term relating to Kua Directions for harmful people in your life is called 'Five Ghosts'. This direction brings in to your life, as the name suggests, harmful people – people gossiping and projecting evil intentions towards you.

MISFORTUNE IN YOUR LIFE – ACCIDENTS, WEALTH, AND ILLNESS

The official Chinese term relating to Kua Directions for misfortune in your life is called 'Six Killings.' It brings about problems with health, loss of wealth, loss of reputation, and general hardship.

TOTAL LOSS IN YOUR LIFE – BANKRUPTCY, LONG TERM ILLNESS AND MAJOR DISASTER

Of the four unfavourable directions, the direction of total loss in your life is the most unfavourable – the most damaging. It brings, as the name suggests, total loss, such as bankruptcy, serious illness and major disasters.

IMPORTANT TO NOTE

It is not always easy to set-up your bed, or desk, in a favourable facing position. Nor is it always easy to sit facing a certain direction in a meeting, or stand facing a certain direction when giving a presentation. The most important thing to note is that as long you are always in one of your four favourable directions, this is ok. You want to always avoid your four unfavourable directions.

CHAPTER 4
KUA NUMBER DIRECTIONS

Let us now take a look at the individual Kua numbers and their individual four favourable and four unfavourable directions over the following pages.

KUA 1

Favourable directions:

Success and prosperity – South East
Good health – East
Love and relationships – South
Personal growth – North

Unfavourable directions:

General bad luck – West
Harmful people – North East
Misfortune – North West
Total loss – South West

KUA 2

Favourable directions:

Success and prosperity – North East

Good health - West

Love and relationships – North West

Personal growth – South West

Unfavourable directions:

General bad luck – East

Harmful people – South East

Misfortune – South

Total loss – North

KUA 3

Favourable directions:

Success and prosperity – South
Good health – North
Love and relationships – South East
Personal growth – East

Unfavourable directions:

General bad luck – South West
Harmful people – North West
Misfortune – North East
Total loss – West

KUA 4

Favourable directions:

Success and prosperity – North
Good health – South
Love and relationships – East
Personal growth – South East

Unfavourable directions:

General bad luck – North West
Harmful people – South West
Misfortune – West
Total loss – North East

KUA 6

Favourable directions:

Success and prosperity – West
Good health – North East
Love and relationships – South West
Personal growth – North West

Unfavourable directions:

General bad luck – South East
Harmful people – East
Misfortune – North
Total loss – South

KUA 7

Favourable directions:

Success and prosperity – North West
Good health – South West
Love and relationships – North East
Personal growth – West

Unfavourable directions:

General bad luck – North
Harmful people – South
Misfortune – South East
Total loss – East

KUA 8

Favourable directions:

Success and prosperity – South West
Good health – North West
Love and relationships – West
Personal growth – North East

Unfavourable directions:

General bad luck – South
Harmful people – North
Misfortune – East
Total loss – South East

KUA 9

Favourable directions:

Success and prosperity – East

Good health – South East

Love and relationships – North

Personal growth – South

Unfavourable directions:

General bad luck – North East

Harmful people – West

Misfortune – South West

Total loss – North West

There you have it – each facing direction for each Kua number and its particular meaning revealed!

CHAPTER 5
USING YOUR KUA NUMBER FOR SITTING AND SLEEPING

SITTING AND SLEEPING POSITIONS

There are two important things to note when determining your facing direction. When sitting, your facing direction is the direction that your face and therefore your eyes are pointing – this is called your sitting face direction.

> *When positioning your bed, you want to position your headboard in your head facing direction.*

However, when lying down your facing direction is the direction the top of your head points towards – this is called your head facing direction.

Therefore, when you are positioning your bed, you want to position your headboard in your head facing direction. This means your bed's headboard is placed along the wall that is in your favourable direction. Examples of both are shown on the following pages.

If you are a Kua number 7 and you wish to sit in your success and prosperity direction, then you want to sit with your face and eyes looking towards the North West. If you are a Kua number 7 and you wish to sleep in your success and prosperity direction, then you want to position your bed's headboard on the North West wall of your bedroom.

It is not always possible to set-up a bed, office, and study desk in your absolute most favourable direction. Your aim is to ensure they are set-up to face at least one of your four favourable directions.

It also depends on what you wish to attract most in your life. If you are seeking romance, this will be one direction, or for good health this will be another direction.

SLEEPING IN YOUR SUCCESS AND PROSPERITY DIRECTION

There is one important thing to note with sleeping in your success and prosperity direction. While sleeping in this direction will bring you success and prosperity, it may also over stimulate you, causing sleeplessness. When we are achieving, creating, being successful, our minds are extremely active. Therefore, you may find trying to sleep in this direction difficult.

IF YOU AND YOUR PARTNER BELONG TO DIFFERENT KUA GROUPS

A common question is what to do sleeping-wise if you and your partner belong to the two different Kua groups. For example, you belong to West Group and your partner belongs to East group. Unfortunately, there is no fix. One of you will be sleeping in an unfavourable direction.

Do not worry about what you cannot fix, but rather concentrate on what you can do...

The decision is entirely up to you and your partner. In olden Chinese times, the decision was made based upon who was the main provider for the family. The bed was set-up in a position to favour this person. The most important thing to note, is to not place your partner in their 'total loss' direction.

If both you and your partner do belong to the same Kua group of numbers it is a definite benefit. You will both be able to tap in to the same type of luck available. However, if you do not belong to the same Kua group, my golden rule in Feng Shui is, 'Do not worry about what you cannot fix, but rather concentrate on what you can do to achieve health, wealth and happiness'.

CHAPTER 6
USING YOUR KUA NUMBER FOR BUSINESS

APPLYING YOUR KUA NUMBER TO MARKETING MATERIAL

In designing any marketing material, you want to ensure your important information – your contact details and your company logo – appear in your favourable directions.

This applies for all marketing material such as business cards, advertisements, website, brochures, flyers, letterheads and compliment slips.

Having your important information in your unfavourable directions will make it harder for people to connect with you and utilise your services. Ultimately, you will be working harder for your income.

IF YOU ARE AN EMPLOYEE

If you are an employee you will most likely have no control over marketing material design. Unfortunately again, there is no fix. It will be pot luck as to whether the company's marketing material coincidentally supports your favourable Kua directions, or not.

IF YOU ARE A BUSINESS OWNER

If you are the business owner, it is your privilege to design your marketing material in your most favourable directions. If you have a large staff-base, or employ a number of salespeople, you may want to design individual business cards for each person in a West or East group layout relevant to each staff member's Kua number.

You may decide to do this if having business cards with two different looks do not bother you. If this does bother you, then my suggestion would be choosing the layout that belongs to the person who brings in the most money for the company. Often this is the owner, director, or sales manager.

On the following page are examples of business card layouts for both West and East groups. Remember, your aim is to ensure your contact details and company logo are positioned in your favourable directions as indicated by the ticks in the examples as follows.

West group business card example

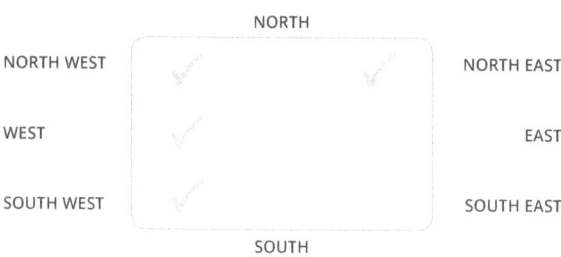

East group business card example

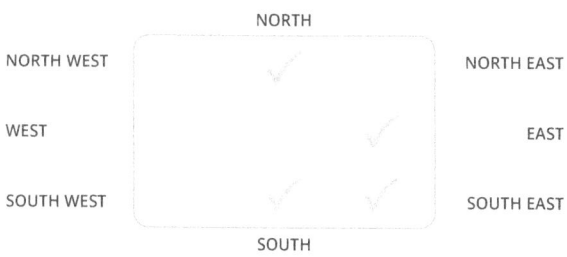

EASY METHOD TO FOLLOW

The easiest method to follow is, for West Kua Directions, to left align all your contact details and place your logo in the top right hand corner. You may choose to utilise the bottom right hand space with a picture.

For East Kua Directions, you can either centre all your contact details, or right align them, or choose a design to incorporate both.

In Feng Shui rounded corners are also always best, for optimum good luck.

CHAPTER 7
YOUR KUA NUMBER IN RELATION TO YOUR HOME

CHOOSING A HOME

Have you ever lived in a home that did not quite feel right? Perhaps there were always setbacks and disappointments in your life, and you could never get ahead?

Your Kua Directions can also be used to determine whether a home will be favourable, or unfavourable for you. Choosing a home that has a facing direction which is compatible to your Kua group of directions will be more auspicious for you.

Meaning, if you are a Kua number 2, 6, 7, or 8, it will be more favourable for you to choose a home that faces West, South West, North West and North East.

Choosing a home that has a facing direction which is compatible to your Kua group of directions will be more auspicious for you.

If you are a Kua number 1, 3, 4, or 9, it will be more favourable for you to choose a home that faces East, South East, North and South.

If you are in a home that does not face one of your favourable directions, you can still set-up your bed, office, and study desk in one of your favourable directions and results will prevail. However, optimum results prevail when your home's facing direction is also compatible with one of your Kua Directions.

The not so easy part is when you and your partner belong to the two different Kua groups. The home in general will always be unfavourable for one of you. This also extends to children, or anyone else living in the home. Again I'll say, do not worry about what you cannot fix, but rather concentrate on what you can do to achieve health, wealth and happiness.

Remember also, Kua Directions is only one school of Feng Shui. If your home is facing an unfavourable direction for you, or you are unable to set-up your bed, or office in one of your favourable directions, there is much else that can be done on a Feng Shui level to help balance the energy in your environment.

*May much abundance
surround you.*

CHAPTER 8
KUA DIRECTIONS FAMILY REFERENCE

REFERENCE TOOL

The following pages have been devised for you to record Kua Directions for each family member, as a quick reference tool.

Name: _____

Gender: _____ **Kua No:** _____

Favourable directions:

Success and prosperity: _____

Good health: _____

Love and relationships: _____

Personal growth: _____

Unfavourable directions:

General bad luck: _____

Harmful people: _____

Misfortune: _____

Total loss: _____

Name: _____

Gender: _____ Kua No: _____

Favourable directions:

Success and prosperity: _____

Good health: _____

Love and relationships: _____

Personal growth: _____

Unfavourable directions:

General bad luck: _____

Harmful people: _____

Misfortune: _____

Total loss: _____

Name: _____

Gender: _____ **Kua No:** _____

Favourable directions:

Success and prosperity: _____

Good health: _____

Love and relationships: _____

Personal growth: _____

Unfavourable directions:

General bad luck: _____

Harmful people: _____

Misfortune: _____

Total loss: _____

Name: _____

Gender: _____ **Kua No:** _____

Favourable directions:

Success and prosperity: _____

Good health: _____

Love and relationships: _____

Personal growth: _____

Unfavourable directions:

General bad luck: _____

Harmful people: _____

Misfortune: _____

Total loss: _____

Name: _____

Gender: _____ **Kua No:** _____

Favourable directions:

Success and prosperity: _____

Good health: _____

Love and relationships: _____

Personal growth: _____

Unfavourable directions:

General bad luck: _____

Harmful people: _____

Misfortune: _____

Total loss: _____

Name: _____

Gender: _____ Kua No: _____

Favourable directions:

Success and prosperity: _____

Good health: _____

Love and relationships: _____

Personal growth: _____

Unfavourable directions:

General bad luck: _____

Harmful people: _____

Misfortune: _____

Total loss: _____

Name: _____

Gender: _____ **Kua No:** _____

Favourable directions:

Success and prosperity: _____

Good health: _____

Love and relationships: _____

Personal growth: _____

Unfavourable directions:

General bad luck: _____

Harmful people: _____

Misfortune: _____

Total loss: _____

Name: _____

Gender: _____ Kua No: _____

Favourable directions:

Success and prosperity: _____

Good health: _____

Love and relationships: _____

Personal growth: _____

Unfavourable directions:

General bad luck: _____

Harmful people: _____

Misfortune: _____

Total loss: _____

ABOUT THE AUTHOR

Loreta Cilfone's career background is in publishing of magazines, newspapers and books. She first stumbled across Feng Shui in 2004, when researching an article for a home magazine, and became a Feng Shui enthusiast immediately. She officially commenced studying and practicing Feng Shui and Chinese Astrology in 2013.

She has undertaken full studies in Perth, on all Feng Shui Schools and Chinese Astrology, and has also attended workshops in Melbourne conducted by renowned Chinese Dato' Joey Yap.

Loreta conducts Feng Shui home party presentations in Perth, whereby she teaches the basics of Feng Shui that can be implemented immediately. She also conducts workshops and Chinese Astrology birth chart readings.

Her business is called Feng Shui Wisdom and she has a website showcasing the most common Feng Shui symbolisation available for purchase.

Loreta is a Professional Member of the Association of Feng Shui Consultants (International) Inc.

CONTACT DETAILS

Loreta Cilfone

0411 531 476

info@fengshuiwisdom.com.au

www.fengshuiwisdom.com.au

Facebook.com/FengShuiWisdom

www.ingramcontent.com/pod-product-compliance
Lightning Source LLC
Chambersburg PA
CBHW070547300426
44113CB00011B/1815